TRACES OF HEAVEN

Carola Moosbach, born in 1957, studied law and lives and works in Cologne, Germany. She has been writing prayers and poems since 1995 and has published three collections of poems in German. In 2000, she was awarded the Prize for New Poetry of the Divine endowed by Hanna Strack. A number of English translations of her texts have appeared in *The Women's Christian Yearbook* and *Worship Live*. Her website is www.carola-moosbach.de

Natalie K. Watson and Giles C. Watson, both born in 1968, live and work in Oxford. Natalie K. Watson is a lecturer at Ripon College Cuddesdon, and editor of *The Women's Christian Yearbook*. Giles C. Watson is a teacher of English and writer of poetry and songs.

Traces of Heaven

Carola Moosbach

Translated by Natalie K. Watson and Giles C. Watson

Published in Great Britain in 2002 by
Society for Promoting Christian Knowledge
Holy Trinity Church
Marylebone Road
London NW1 4DU

British Library Cataloguing-in-Publication Data

A catalogue record for this book is available from the British Library

ISBN 0–281–05394–4

Typeset by Wilmaset Ltd, Birkenhead, Wirral
Printed in Great Britain by
Omnia Books, Glasgow

Contents

Introduction

In this collection of prayers, Carola Moosbach takes her readers on a journey of discovery. She invites us to find 'traces of heaven' where we do not expect them. She shares her own experiences of circling 'godwards', of struggling with open questions, with her own suffering and that of others, and of the deep joy of finding traces of God in unexpected places. Carola Moosbach retraces parts of her own journey of rediscovering prayer, of learning to pray afresh and of finding a new way to God and with God. To Carola Moosbach God is the nourishing bread that wants to be shared among those who need her. As one who has discovered the love of God in her own life, she invites others to share her journey, to travel their own journeys with God and towards God.

Carola Moosbach speaks of God as One who is indeed wholly other from conventional forms of religion and church, from religion as a means of condoning violence or a comfortable way to ease one's conscience. God is beyond what can be said or even thought, God is too present, too absent to be confined to preconceived ideas. And yet there is the challenge to search for new ways of speaking about God, breaking free from language and images that have blocked the dignity of women and men as human beings in the image of God.

She discovers new images of God as her powerful ally, as gentle lover, as the one who suffers wherever human beings suffer, as incorrigible dreamer of justice and love. In her poems and prayers, Carola Moosbach expresses her experience of being a survivor of sexual abuse as part of her search for new images of the divine and new forms of praying. While some poems reflect the experience of beauty and joy, others are cries of helplessness and anger about injustice and suffering. It is a deep honesty that characterizes Carola Moosbach's writing, an honesty about her own feelings and also an honesty with God. In her poems, we discover a mature loving relationship with God: she speaks to God, argues with her, laughs, cries and sings, or as

Dorothee Soëlle says: 'Carola Moosbach praises God without lying.'
This mature relationship is deeply personal and at the same time
public and political; it has consequences that affect all aspects of daily
life and allow the whole of life, with its different experiences, to be part
of this loving and healing relationship. God wants to be encountered as
a person who desires our love, our prayers, our questions. This en-
counter happens in the tension between a familiar loving relationship
and deep awe for the abundance of God's being. God is no longer an
'almighty father', the graven image of patriarchal idolatry, but the one
who is there as a friend, as a lover, as one who challenges and offers a
place to rest in times of trouble as well as space for joy and celebration,
one who is both far away and nearby.

However, it is not easy consolation that Carola Moosbach offers. In
her prayers she gives a voice to those whom traditional prayer books
have often denied it. She does not hesitate to ask painful questions, to
cry out for help and protection. And she seeks new images of the
divine, a new female–God language. This new God language is liberat-
ing, healing and nourishing, and as such is in stark contrast to the
patriarchal images of God as the all-powerful and overpowering
father, which it seeks to challenge and to replace.

Prayer can mean to find God, to make room for the Other, in the
midst of the business of good days and bad days. There are days and
nights that pass by, just killing time and silencing the torment of
painful memories when God seems absent, even dead. And then there
are those surprising moments, perhaps over a cup of coffee, when the
conversation turns to God and all of a sudden God herself is present.

Chapter 1, *Reaching Out to Heaven in the Midst of the Day*, offers
prayers for every day, prayers that can be a point of refocusing while
roaming through the valley of the week.

There are those times when prayer is easy and God seems the obvious
place to turn. And there are those times when all we can manage are a
few chunks of prayer thrust out into the seeming void in the vague hope
that there is One who hears. These 'times of trouble' are part of the
journey of rediscovering God and growing into a new mature and
honest relationship with God and with others. The words of someone
like Carola Moosbach, found in Chapter 2, *I Will Take Courage and
Breathe in Happiness*, offer a valuable resource for times when whole
days are spent crying, when the world shrinks to the walls of a hospital
room, when the same scars break open time and again.

Prayer can also be a way to mark those special occasions, the birth of a child, holidays, changes in life's circumstances or meetings with those who share similar experiences. Those are times when God may *grant us the lightness of her blessing*. Chapter 3 is a collection of such prayers for special occasions. What makes these occasions special is that they mark the high points and low points that are part of human life, entrances and exits, welcomes and times of taking a deep breath before a new step, and times to change gear. They are also times to reflect on what really matters, to reassess our own goals and those of the world around us.

Prayer also means *circling Godwards*, seeking and finding a very personal relationship with God. Carola Moosbach does not provide an easy recipe for pious happiness, but speaks of the difficulty in seeking God and the joy of finding traces of her, fragments of faith and love in unexpected places. The texts in Chapter 4 speak about crossing boundaries, being on our way sometimes through a dark spring, finding miracles even for the satisfied.

Yet prayer is not restricted to a personal relationship with God, but takes its place in all kinds of situations of personal and public life. *That There Was a Home to be Found* is a collection of *prayers and open questions* that forms Chapter 5: honest questions about issues such as violence against women and children, or the situation of Jerusalem as a divided holy city. Such open questions can be a disturbance of peaceful piety; they can also be a challenge to change direction, to move on full of courage or to demand that what is wanted is indeed truth. Carola Moosbach makes it clear that God, found in her search for a new language, is too precious to leave to the representatives of patriarchal idolatry and social injustice, but that her love permeates all situations and is present as a constant challenge and disruption to pious complacency and the condoning of the abuse of power and violence.

Prayer has always been part of the Christian tradition, and Carola Moosbach sees her own writing in creative and constructive dialogue with the tradition that she challenges at the same time. The book concludes with Chapter 6, *Days Coloured with God: Prayers Throughout the Christian Year*. God spreads her loving and disturbing presence through every day, through special days, through pain and happiness. Carola Moosbach, Christian and writer, feminist and poet, challenges us to rethink the meaning, to find meaning and essentially God's presence, as well as our own lives in those traditional holy days of the

Christian year: Advent, Holy Week, Easter, Pentecost through to All Souls' Day.

Traces of Heaven is a book to 'learn to pray' with, both for those for whom prayer is a familiar experience and for those who may be circling towards God after a long break or perhaps for the first time.

Natalie K. Watson

ONE

Reaching Out to Heaven in the Midst of the Day: Prayers for Every Day

MORNING PRAYER FOR A GOOD DAY

I thank you God
for the groping grey and the hesitant silence
of the beginning
I thank you for the blessings of the first cup of coffee
for the bread the honey and the cigarette to go with it
I delight God
in the fresh breeze
the rushing clouds above the city
in the roofs still shining with the dew of the night
today I will face up to the day
with light hands and feet I will do what is necessary
attune myself to what is important
today I will impress upon the time my mind my being
I will not be afraid of the coming hours
today I will delight God
in life and to be part of your creation

MORNING PRAYER FOR A BAD DAY

The hour of morning
lies in my mouth numb like cotton wool
far away behind glass is the world
this day will be hard
I do not know why where to what purpose
Yet I shall begin
empty hours stretch towards me
make me weary already now
with a deaf soul I speak dumb words
in your direction God
are you there?
Even if I cannot feel anything today
even if I have nothing to show for today
no plan no strength no goal for the day
are you there anyway God?
Say yes for me

PRAYER AT NOON

In the midst of the day
reaching out to heaven
with short arms
but at least
beyond time purpose and goals
a fleeting glance
at least

In the midst of the day
making space for the Other
eating and not forgetting
who made it
laughing and praying
with an impetuous mouth
but at least

EVENING PRAYER FOR A GOOD DAY

Said yes
and even no
at the right time

Met people
and made a home
in the right place

Did work
and knew what it was for
tasted life
and was understood
in the depths

My weary head
laid in your darkness
and the open questions
in your wrinkly heart
restward

EVENING PRAYER FOR A BAD DAY

Time
killed
dead
pain
silenced
to death
said
God
is dead
said
God

NIGHT PRAYER

What business of mine are the stars
what meaning is there in the moon
whether out there shining or not
helpless I drift through the shadows
drift through my fears and my dreams
no cry comes out of my mouth

To talk
with whom?
to cry
why?
to pray
where to?
the darkness casts light on the truth
nothing is certain not really
not even you God
or are you?

SATURDAY DESIRES

If only there was one to affirm
my doing
writing thinking moving letters here and there
that it may have had meaning in the end
If only there was one to draw me
into the light for a few hours
just laughing talking walking by the water
If only there was one to give me
time roses and stars
If only there was one to speak
the right word

BLESSING FOR A HOME

A safe place
warmth and light
silence
books music kitchen table talk
the view out of the window into the distance
space for this one or that one
this or that
life full of colours
a den if necessary
home
meanwhile

ON THE BALCONY

we were sitting talking
I don't know why
all of a sudden about you
God
hesitant slightly embarrassed
and quietly
the words fragile
near
were you to us God
for an instant
very clearly

FRAGILE DAYS

Hardly dare I
say it
there is nothing
to reach out to with bare hands
just that light
the old trees people the playground
everything is just right
today
I feel I breathe
happiness that is you God

WOMAN'S BLESSING

I am a woman
I think feel work
struggle

I am a woman
I cry feel laugh
dream

I am a woman
I write
bring forth words

I am a woman
in her image
by her strength

EVERYDAY PRAYER

Roaming through the valley of the week
with wind in my back
in the everyday grey
drawing
on the gentle green of your light
steering
my feet in your direction
opening
my hands for your blessing
putting the pains on your breast God
being allowed
to be weary
in the embrace of your clouds

TWO

I Will Take Courage and Breathe in Happiness: Prayers for Times of Trouble

IN HOSPITAL

the world shrinks very small
becomes the glance a glass of water
the clock
on the wall three hours' sleep to go
until the morning then at last coffee
later the procession of doctors through the room
a quick glance sentences said but not looked at
questions asked but not heard
and I gaze out of the window behind it the usual
sun and rain who cares in here music of fear
life and death and eating and sleeping
and waiting and hoping then again fear next to me
one is crying but I cannot comfort her don't have enough myself
to go on so eyes shut and music on the ears
that easy that difficult

In hospital
sometimes a few chunks of prayer thrust
into the chalk white light heard no answer but visitors came
again and again
spoke into friendly eyes
was that you God?

BLESSING FOR ONE WHO IS SICK

Into your fear
a calm voice

Against your pain
a comforting hand

For your hope
words of strength

Into your anger
no wise sayings

Against your boredom
a beautiful movie with vanilla ice-cream

For your happiness
days coloured with God

PRAYER OF UNBELIEF

for those like me
who really want to know
what is true and not
to look for cheap consolation
who cannot trust anyone
and anything and the truth is
that I am scared afraid of dying
of life that fades away without trace
the truth is
that we cannot know it
only hopes shyly written into the sand
with hesitant hands
and the truth is
possibly greater
than we can ever comprehend

PRAYER CALL

Oh help me
to pray
oh help me
to jump
over the edge
of knowledge
help me to go to the land
beyond words
but only then
when everything has been said
oh help me
to be silent
God

WARNING! PAIN

With one like me one has nothing but trouble
constantly this pain these unpleasant truths
horrible childhood stories about the father
the rapist the mother not much better
who would like to hear that possibly even on Sundays
the childhood faith might vanish
the chronic Christian smile might freeze sometimes
in your face the old certainties begin to break
and new ways of amusement might lead into the void
this pain blows up everything and then this anger
but also strength in all that inaccessible suspicious
whole days spent crying that goes deep very deep
into the eye of the storm there is something
some call it God

NOCTURNAL MUSINGS

I'd rather not
think about it
but it is all around me I'd rather not
talk about it
but it chokes me I'd rather not
feel so much
but it hurts so much I'd rather
be able to say
everything
at least to you God

TIME AND AGAIN

it breaks open the pain burns
itself into me deeper and deeper the crater of wounds
open themselves deeper and deeper spit out
blood and death in my throat
the eyes of him the father fresh
very fresh within me fear disgust
the usual but how
can I cope with it how
live with it and yet
I do it
survive the break-ins
time and again

FOR ONE WHO TOOK HER LIFE

I know how you tried sister
how you cried for help silently and out loud
you searched for life in your own way I know
survival was not enough for you
tumbling here and there
these images pain for life
that was unbearable I know
and then
you jumped
into nothing or something who can say
you were tired simply tired I know
your father brother neighbour or whoever it was
used you and then cast you away
you felt like dirt in the end I know
but
we miss you are you listening?
we miss you speaking out saying the truth
fighting struggling and crying if necessary
but
that is not enough I know

TIME TO GRIEVE

No I will not smile today
just so that you feel better
No I don't want a prescription no distraction
shopping positive thinking booking a flight anywhere

No I will not smile today
just to keep up appearances
sad I want to be and cry
the pain out of my soul

AT LEAST

There is so much lacking
so terribly much
happiness and human closeness
life and lightness

Hope at least
words at least
traces at least
I need from you
don't forget that God

FOR COMFORT

send me I don't know what
perhaps a glance that does not turn away
time much time is what I need light words and deep words
tears being able to cry at last but then
not to remain alone
send me music that the scars
may close the fractured heart beats on
in wide open space held together
by your hand of stars softly God
very softly

LOVE HOWEVER (1 Corinthians 13.1–3)

Strange word of angels
empty word of lies
distant word of pain
love
where if not from you
how if not myself
whom if not you

COURAGE IN BETWEEN

Living to live my life is what I want
even if some things are lacking in it
even if I do not know what is yet to come
even if it hurts and it hurts a lot sometimes
I want to live notwithstanding
no longer wait for better days to come
no longer simply kill time
living to live my life is what I want
to practise saying yes and not to forget saying no
I want to take courage and breathe in happiness
sometimes

THREE

Grant Us God the Lightness of Your Blessing: Prayers for Special Occasions

BLESSING FOR A CHILD I

On the occasion of the birth of Felix Hammelsbeck

Everything you shall be able to say
everything you shall be able to ask
learn play dance sing
laugh paint play hoolahoop
You shall look into the eyes of those
who love you with warmth and protection
Hands shall hold you
taking your first steps
and everything shall come to life
the gifts that lie dormant within you
In the evening you shall be tired and satisfied
protected in restful darkness
sleep dream make plans
looking forward to the new day

BLESSING FOR A CHILD II

Child with the ancient look
at the age of eight already sold to a brothel
and you child emaciated and you
the one who is battered only screaming and silence
around you and the television is on
from morning until evening

Child with the speechless look
peered far too early into the abyss
too soon lost the power to dream
and nothing hoped since then
nothing believed
not in yourself and not in anyone

I do not know child what will happen to you
if God will find human arms
to carry you
a safe place where you can grow
and rest a place where you can feel
whether you believe it or not
that God wanted you child and loves
just you

TRAVEL BLESSING

May you have a good journey
a pleasant conversation
an exciting book to read on your way
open eyes for the wide open space
open ears for what is new
calm amongst blowing horns ringing bells shouting
time for the stars of the strange skies
with safe steps on distant paths

HOLIDAY PRAYER

It takes time
until the days get used to the different rhythm
and swing slowly according to the metre of retreat
It takes time
until the everyday worries find rest
the soul stretched out and liberated
from the dust of the year

Help me into this different time God
teach me the joy and the fresh look
at what is beautiful
I want to feel the wind and taste the air
I want to hear the sound of your laughter
and in all that
your silence

PRAYER FOR MOVING HOUSE

For the last time
wiping over the sink
dragging the last boxes through empty rooms
a hard time it was here
but with you God

For the last time
driving through the narrow street
last familiarities here I used to buy bread
there the paper but no looking back
with melancholy

For the first time
in the new bedroom strangely
folding up the bed
first habits develop even
around you God
move in with me here you familiar
one from a distance

OBITUARY (for one leaving the church)

Tell us
what you missed
tell us
what bothered you
don't just leave
please
tell us what you think and also
what you believe and no longer believe
whatever you feel
anger disappointment indifference
tell us
do

WELCOME (for one joining the church)

Bring along your longing
your wishes and your dreams
bring your new look
into our fatigue

Bring along your story
your ways with God and without
your questions and your doubts
into our security

Bring along your confidence
your hope against the stream
your courage to be different
into our anxiety

FINDING TRACES (for a self-help group)

Here we sit scar on scar
pain on pain
here we sit sharing
hope and tears
anger and strength
here we sit looking for
ways and traces
burnt out dreams
here we sit finding
life

FLYER (for a vigil)

Yes we are still there
even if it does not make the paper
yes really we are still dreaming
greater than money and your own home
further than the next holiday
yes we are still standing here
for justice and peace
against torture and arms trade
yes we do think it is worth it
even if it does not add up
yes we still stand up
for life we it call God

FORTIES

For Ulrike Gebhardt on her 40th birthday

Foundations laid
points set on course
stones carried
reached this goal left behind that one
first treasures found
first treasures lost
strength bundling up
some things now or never
dreams still growing
into the sky only sometimes
open end

PRAYER FOR THE DEAD

We are thinking of you
we are talking about you
we are mourning you
today and again and again
you shall be alive in us
through our words
through our hope
through our love for you
today and again and again
we miss you
so much
God give us tears
God become our strength
God hide you keep you
softly

SUNDAY PRAYER

Tell us God about the beginning of the world
how you gave birth to the stars
in a wild dance and interwove humans
with sky and earth
Whisper your silver dreams
into our weary everyday ears
Tell us your stories anew
about searching and finding about reaping and sharing
about the promised land behind time
Your truth draw into our rent hearts
speak your love into our loneliness God
and your faithfulness into our frightened lives
Grant us God the lightness of your blessing

FOUR

About Circling Godwards: Prayers of Seeking and Finding

I WILL NOT LEAVE YOU (Matthew 15.21–28)

God I call you by your name
I run after you whether you want it or not
I won't rest until you answer me God
nothing and no one will take that away from me
not even you
talk to me God be moved
by my suffering be touched by my cry
I want to argue with you and fight if necessary
I want to take your word for your love
I won't be fended off by cold truths
and narrow boundaries
never will I believe that you are so far away God
as it seems
never will I believe that I do not count for you
your silence I want to turn into nearness
my trust will overcome you God
you will bless me and become everything for me
in everything

PRAYER REPORT (Luke 11.5–13)

Quick words colliding
against the wall
icy darkness eating its way through
to the heart
nothing flying into wide open space nothing flowing
over the edge
God just a word dead childish word
no asking and begging
no searching and finding
just tears
streaming nevertheless
you know where

CASHING UP (Matthew 18.21–35)

He had the choice
he has made his decision
up to this day he does not face up to his guilt
pretends that nothing happened
he raped me
abused the daughter for years
he enjoyed my weakness
my fear and my stupidity

Don't talk to me
about forgiveness

I wanted to die
not remember
I numbed myself as much as I could
hated myself and despised him
even today I feel sick
when I think of him
half my life I needed
to acquit myself

Don't talk to me
about forgiveness
tell me
about God's justice

OPEN QUESTION (Matthew 2.13–18)

No one
was told in a dream
to take me away
no matter where
no plan of salvation
was implemented
to protect me
from my father
what then is
this one child
and what its rescue
God?

ATTEMPTED RECONCILIATION WITH MYSELF
(Luke 6.36–37)

I was still a toddler and I thought
that was just what fathers are like
later I wanted to resist him
but he was stronger and there was no one else
for me
then I forgot everything except for the hatred
this merciless look
through his eyes I looked at myself
and was just a bit of trash

Now it is time to make peace at last
with myself
to understand who I was and who I am
slowly to make my home in the land of the humans
And my father?
Him I leave to you God
I know your answer will be clear
and he will hear it
he will have to

READY TO FIGHT (Romans 12.21)

I will not
become like you
I will not be drawn
into the fouling smell of your guilt
in abuse numbness and lies
of your life
you will not have destroyed me
forever
I can stick it out longer
my life will have meaning and dignity
grace and depth
that will be my retaliation against you
with the help of
God

IN PRAISE OF LAMENT (Lamentations 3.1–44)

With all my strength
to break through
the wall of silence
with pain and anger
bricks of walls to loose
out of the mouth of stone
to cry out
the truth
possibly into the void
despite all
to set out to jump
into the saving
You

WANTED URGENTLY (Luke 15.8–10)

Invisible behind walls of numbness
buried deeply in a hiding place of lies
I was hidden under the gravel of my fear
nothing and no one could find me there
not even myself

You God were just a word a dead one
poisoned by my father to the brim
I had nothing to do with you
until you began to look out for me
why on earth
at first there was just a weak vibration far away
a strange sound from somewhere
then suddenly light in all corners
what had been right at the bottom you turned upside down
just to find me
why on earth
screaming was the light
of the truth but also comforting
and healing
so urgently you need me then
my happiness
so important we are for you
and so great is the joy we share

CHANGE OF POWER (Ezekiel 34.1–16)

She who was supposed to nurture me
with warmth
took advantage of
my love
planted within me her pain

He who was supposed to protect me
with tenderness
gloated over
my fear
felt strong in my weakness

Those who were supposed to tell me
about you God
talked about my sin
made me small and filthy
the body the girl child

She who was a stranger to me
her name poisoned
pushed everything aside
parents clerics stories of lies
she swept them out of my eyes out of my mind
made room for herself comfort fresh light green
by my side

TURNING POINT (Acts 9.1–9)

No voice of God
spoke no angel
appeared by my side
no light dazzled me
or enlightened
but
the ice was broken the pain
thawed into tears and doors
opened and led into the open air
life
now stands on firmer ground
with roots growing into the deep
and meaning
steadily circling
godwards

SECOND ATTEMPT (Luke 14.16–24)

At first I thought
there was a way
out of myself
into wide open space
truth enlightenment and meaning
I wanted to find
in my own strength

Only when I stood there empty handed
and knew nothing at all any more
only when I had nothing more to lose
and had to rely on others
I allowed myself to be picked up by you
so you were not my first choice God
possibly you thought the same about me
never mind – the main thing is to be invited

IN SPITE OF ALL THAT (2 Corinthians 12.1–10)

It is you alone God
who can strike sparks even out of tears
who turns cries into words of healing
It is you alone God
this stream of joy sometimes
inexplicable tenderness longing
burnt right into the heart
It is you alone God
who turns weakness into strength
makes my life rich
You do all of these things
but despite all that I am bleeding
no one soothes this scar
not even you God
can do everything

SCARRED AND ALIVE (Luke 13.10–17)

With a broken eye
I see some things more sharply and deeper
into the dark
with a trashed heart
I feel over the edge
beyond my sadness
Upright I walk with wounded feet
with God's strength in my back
the soul bleeds
but no longer unto death
the pains speak
me into the world
he has not
broken me
out of this scar flows
even
life

DARK SPRING (John 12.24)

Out of my pain have grown depths of words

my tears have thrust their roots
in the wind

plentiful harvest carries my darkness

some cries
have become answers

INTERIM REPORT (Mark 10.17–27)

No house and no money
not even a car
un–
employed
hardly of use at all
rich
with words
does not pay
people
love
too little
in need of
God
from the ground
found
life
with empty hands

BASIC QUESTIONS (Matthew 4.1–11)

The main thing is
to be healthy?
I won't ever be any more

The main thing is
to be beautiful?
Once upon a time if at all

The main thing is
to have fun?
Well yes

The main thing is
to have work?
I have got some but it's not paid

The main thing is
to have money?
It will be enough somehow

The main thing is
to live
with meaning to the full

CALL SIGN (Luke 8.1–3)

You look for me and call me God
but where to and where from is the question
and what do you want from me
when you scream and whisper
and get on my nerves
with this nagging desire
and numb emptiness – maybe that was the wrong direction
no use running after anyone
and no use parroting anything
every now and then some traces others had already been there
and saw your smile your love
from which everything comes is the sign
but what does that mean now
for me and how can I
in my own way walk in God's direction?

JUST BEFORE (Romans 8.26)

it was very simple the words
ready everywhere
glory honour and praise or
fear crying and anger who cares
the main thing is: to God but now
silence stony silence
the words wobbly all of a sudden
wrong far too small far too big
it is time to wait
simply to wait
what for?
It will turn out

THIRD WAY (1 Peter 5.5)

Not above and not below
not better and not worse
not smaller and not greater
than the others you want me God
I am meant to be simply human

Not creeping and bent
not childish and fatalistic
not immaculate and infallible
I need to stand before you God
I can be simply human

Not deaf to your questions and word
not blind to the other ways
not numb in the light of screaming injustice
I want to live in you God
I want to be simply human

ASKING BACK (Micah 8.6)

I am supposed to keep your word God
but what is your word and how can I distinguish it
from human opinions and male delusion
from the trash of the times and lies

I am supposed to be humble before you God
but how can I do that without humiliating myself
to take you seriously God and honour you
with dignity

Why am I supposed to do
what you demand of me God
I do not believe in the torments of hell
and eternal condemnation
in bonus points to be gathered
in a heavenly account
why then God if not out of love
but that is the hardest of all

SPECIAL OFFER (Isaiah 43.1)

You have chosen me God
to be human
would I be alive otherwise?
You call me by my name God
and you wait for a reply
a smile a question a lament perhaps
there is no right or wrong
You make an offer God
which is neither free of charge nor without obligation
when I reject you still love me you strange one
but you are missing something
there is this or that or the other
on which I can set my heart instead
but then I am missing something
You clever one

DISTURBANCE OF THE PEACE (Romans 8.14)

Can't forget you
can't ignore you permanently
nuisance tender
God your strength
drives me draws me
here and there demands
words and deeds disturb me
from the edge wanting this and that
then again far away unfathomable
unrest you bring and joy
at the same time

ON MY WAY (John 4.5–14)

So far you are not streaming
so far you are not bubbling
here and there a few drops
on the hand the dry tongue
no more

So far I am waiting
so far I am looking for you
out there in there
what do I know
but the thirst for life
for you God
that I know

MIRACLE FOR THE SATISFIED (John 6.1–15)

Here you do not need anyone
to multiply the bread
we already have enough and more than enough
of everything
satisfied and yet hungry
full to the brim and yet empty
we remain searching
for who how and what
do I know what we are lacking
only you have got it God

And is that not a miracle
trace of heaven for the satisfied
that nothing can replace you God?

(HI)STORY OF FAITH (John 20.24–29)

Proofs I have none
in magic tricks I do not believe
sometimes in miracles
when God begins to circle all of a sudden
life breaks open joy
bubbles new hope
out of nothing a cheeky laughter
against all appearances
then again doubts asking again thinking
looking for traces again and again
practising wonderment
that's how it is

INTERCESSION (Ephesians 1.15–20a)

Our faith
let it grow God
thrust roots
in your midst

Our eyes
let them speak God
become a reflection
of your love

Our joy
let it dance God
on firm ground
of your strength

CROSSING THE BOUNDARY (Mark 12.41–44)

Half heartedness
turn into wholeness of soul
narrow mindedness
turn into broad perspective
into bouncing
turn our staggering
let us be without measure
in our hope
what seems impossible easily
drawn into the sky
with wasteful abundance dreaming
towards you

DAY OF WONDERS (Isaiah 60.2)

I don't know how nor why
and not even how long
she stays and whence out of the void
it comes very lightly
her breath brushes against my soul
nothing great nothing small
comes flying there very quietly
she touches me draws me into her saving warming feathers
and light blue being joyful

It comes stays and goes as it wills
free like a bird and connected
it might have to do with God
wonderful protection

WITHOUT ASKING WHY (Psalm 66.1–5)

a spark sparked
out of a smile perhaps
of divine longing
for more
created milky ways of stars worlds of darkness
light poured out of nothing
everything streams and bubbles
flowers and flourishes
just like that
even the words
rise up from the ground
ground of joy springtime
living all
without asking why

SKETCH IN THE SAND (Exodus 33.17b–23)

Your beauty
unbearable
too light too dark for us

Your mystery
unfathomable
hidden and visible everywhere

Your proximity
unenforceable
sometimes you give yourself to us

Your love
to be shared

YOUR WILL (Isaiah 61.1–3, 10–11)

You want to be our direction
a current against the stream
and a voice amidst a chatter of lies

You want to be our freedom
courage to stand on our own feet
and wings amidst a swamp of sorrows

You want to be our healing
colour in our multi-coloured monotony
and a Band-Aid for our scars

You want to be all in all
your will be done
wherever possible

NOTHING SHALL PART US [Song]

Nothing shall part us
from your love
nothing shall discourage us
make us afraid
praying and silence
singing and laughter
everything flows to you

Tune: Nada te Turbe (Taizé)

STANDING ORDER (Matthew 5.13–16)

To pass on the news about you
savoury and sweet
dark and light
to share your truth
as love
among the people
to be your glance
all around
to be your scream
from below
to demand
your justice
and to practise
to speak words of light
to learn
on your grounds

WITH HEART AND MOUTH (Luke 12.48)

With heart and mouth
I will continue to write
the grand world poem of God

With deed and strength
I will continue to work
God's wildest dreams
for us

With head and hand
I will help to heal
the earth
the wounded body of God

FIVE

That There Was a Home to be Found:
Prayers and Open Questions

LITTLE CHURCH HISTORY (Romans 13.1–7)

In the beginning it might even have been clever
so many had already been killed and therefore they promised
to be loyal to the state and obey those in power
at some point they really began to believe
that God gives power to the mighty and will punish all those
who turn against them
yet later they themselves were those in power
Lords over good and evil over heaven and earth
they could only think about power from the top down
with God at the top then the king as his vicar
below the other men and down at the end
the women animals and other nothings

They ruled invented and shaped the world
in their image
every now and then there was war women were burnt as witches
wild ones struck down and all those who were different
thought differently or believed differently from them were kept small
with swords and words from scripture
with torture persecution and lies
God had nothing to say among them any more even Jesus
did not fare much better who wanted to end like he did and who live
    like that
obsessed with God without protection and in poverty that would not
    happen to them
they would not be as lovingly stupid
instead it grew well the church continued to expand
in the wrong direction

but then the problems came
the people did not quite believe them any more and those in power
had other servants now who were more colourful and everything was
   possible
with them as long as it was fun

The poor rich church found itself on the margins
when it mattered it now preferred to keep silent and was always
a bit for it and a bit against
no one really knew how to go on
only God had not quite given up yet
lit up beacons and some even in church
nothing is decided yet the end is open

CONTRADICTION (Numbers 12.1–15)

How could you men dare
talk her sick
lie her small
How could you deny God's truth
that was dancing when Miriam spoke and sang
her song of liberation
How could you dare lock up God
in the language of rulers and talk of fear
use God for stories of hatred
of impure women
spat at and restricted to silence that is what you did to them
And what are you doing today?

Don't even think God is waiting for your permission
to burn in whoever she wants
don't even think we are waiting for your permission
to rise up and break out
of this church which will die
if you don't get it at last

DREAMS OF A CHURCH (Galatians 3.28)

That there was a home to be found
for those who ask true questions
and have unconquerable dreams because they are greater
than all calculations and stronger
than any laws of the market

That there was a place to share
about our doubts pain and hope
about new thoughts and old truths
a place of courage and of justice
not of tranquillizers and false securities

That there was a voice to be heard
behind the voices
more beautiful than any music and full to the brim
with love
a spoke in the wheel of the world
and direction in the whirl of the times

UNHEARD WORDS OF GOD (Amos 5.21–24)

I despise your holy wars
your crusades make me puke
don't even pretend you were killing for my sake
as if it was me who desires rape and murder

I hate the way you worship money
your obsession with progress I cannot stand
don't even pretend there are no victims
on your altars of stock exchange and motorways

I laugh about your pious pretences
your empty words I don't want to hear
don't even pretend I am your property
rather make sure that my love can flow
everywhere on earth

TIME CHECK

When bombs are all of a sudden called air strikes
and supposedly no one was burnt in the fire
when refugees are suddenly welcome among us
of course only the ones from the right side
then I know: it is war now

When politicians begin to look like statesmen
and won't speak of parties but only of the nation
when some are good others can only be bad
and the end justifies the means again
then I know: it is war.

When somehow everything turned out differently
than the war lords had imagined
when afterwards everything is worse
and no one wants to have known that before
then they say: no more war!
Until next time

OH JERUSALEM

Besieged destroyed rebuilt
fought over torn apart bleeding
out of all pores the stones cry out
to heaven yet want to remain
a home for God but how
should that be possible a place
to pray for all God visible
in the smiles of the children no more enemies
no shooting and bombing no hatred
on all sides and blood on the hands
when will you show yourself God
in peace?

WANTED: TRUTH (Jeremiah 16.23–29)

So many things have been put into God's mouth
the words twisted and turned
until they fitted human plans of power violence and war
from Calvary to Auschwitz
whom should we believe then and what?

The truth might not even exist
spread out into all directions moved inside or searched for
with the stars in the sky
the new prophets predict the movements of the stock exchange
and soothsayers this end of the world or that
otherwise they think positively say what is pleasant
announce happiness with the lightness of the tongue

And you God?
Do you still talk to us at all and if so
why so quietly why not with power and fire
clearly and understandable for all
And we?
Who wants to hear God's truths
and who of us has got the guts
to say them?

DISCOURAGEMENT (Isaiah 5.1–7)

Justice
does not exist
peace
does not pay
dreams
burst
we are tired God what about you?
Your cry
drowned
your misery
far away
your name
unknown

YOU ARE THE ONE (Matthew 25.40–45)

You are the one your body
strays in the freezing cold
hungry and thirsty
for bread and justice

You are the one your pain
numbed and denied
disposed of on the graveyard
of fun culture

You are the one your blood
shed daily
for our wealth
for lust after money and the market laws.

You are the one Your cry God
of the earth

INVERSION (Luke 18.1–8)

Just imagine
that God was the widow and not the judge
in this story
begging persistently angry whatever
she came running along
demanding rights her rights from us
for the odd ones out and those without means
for the refugees victims of torture and street kids
just imagine
we were those in power
corrupt complacent and arrogant like that judge
indifferent with regard to others and God
but she would simply not give up
would bend our ears with her justice
a complete pain in the neck just imagine
which one of us would want to hear
that?

REPORT ON MY SORROWS (Matthew 6.25–34)

The lilies birds and butterflies
may be cared for
but how many people have to fight all their lives
for the mouldy daily bread
for fouling fruits and cast of rags
from the litter of the rich ones
Their days remain hungry no one gives them anything
Certainly not in their sleep
I wonder if they still believe in fairy tales.
I certainly don't and of course I worry
about myself and further still
about tomorrow the day after
and beyond

I know it is not your fault God
You send lilies bread and fruit in abundance
and also strength courage and stories of hope
about a good life for all
about your justice
I know that is a lot quite a lot
everything else is our concern
at least until further notice

NOT TO FORGET (Mark 14.3–9)

To live and yet to be mindful of dying
dying and despite everything to hope for life
to regale God with words of joy
or do you think God is not in need of us?
Comfort and strength in her defeat
eyes and ears for her treasures
no requests no lament no questions today
just melodious sounds aroma and tenderness
for the One the Other
not to calculate if it pays
not to be rational and to invest in what is probable
to waste time on what is useless
to have open ears for what is flighty
and to set hope on what is lost

REPENTANCE FOR WOMEN (Revelation 3.15–16)

The arguments
not to evade
to speak loud and clearly
even when it matters
the false smile
off the face
and to call
the crude jokes what they are
not to run away
into an inner emigration
not to be afraid
of power
and never to forget
who created us
in her image

AND YET (Mark 10.35–45)

You can't promise anything
and yet
you demand everything
you have a premonition of what is to come
and yet
you remain faithful to yourself
you feel entirely deserted
and yet
you cry out to God
you are entirely unreasonable
and yet
you convince

PERSPECTIVES (Matthew 20.1–16a)

Performance matters
only sometimes

Those who do not work
should still eat

The weak ones in the centre
the strong ones by their side

Incorrigible dreamer
God

SIGN OF THE TIMES (Luke 17.20–30)

It has long started already
God is already drawn in
here there and over yonder
new life draws forth
from dust dirt and misery
some rise up
from lethargy and emptiness
some break out
from gluttony and coldness
some turn around
We can all jump into this river
the water will carry to the end
and become a beginning for us perhaps
we stream on further and further
into the flooding light
perhaps
God's truth will thaw the way
melt away all injustice
and love will have the last word

SIX

Days Coloured with God:
Prayers Through the Christian Year

Advent Sunday

ADVENT QUESTIONS (Romans 13.11–12)

What
are we really waiting for
and what are the things
we need more
than ever
and how
should there be a beginning
of what
and who
still hopes at all
for what
and when
will it break
this day
of light
and who
still believes in it?

Second Sunday in Advent

ADVENT FOR GROWN-UPS (Luke 21.25–33)

If
the sky breaks open
really open
the Other breaks through
can't be overlooked
dark light terrible
beautiful
what would that be like
if
not?

Third Sunday in Advent

ADVENT CALL (Matthew 11.2–6)

God share your love
with us your light your joy
let us be
enter our lives
on the edge in the middle and everywhere
you want to be
for us

God share your dreams
with us into your mystery
draw us deep
your sign we shall
be already here and now
and wide open space
within us

Fourth Sunday in Advent

CHRISTMAS WISHES

Hopefully
it will be all right this year
hopefully we won't argue
he won't start drinking
in the morning already
hopefully
the children will be happy
they will play and not run away
who knows where
hopefully I won't cry

Christmas Eve

EVERY YEAR

again
silence falls even
the tram is quiet
in the darkness the lights
do not really light up
for me
it is another one that counts
child that I was
I hear her cry
alone
with you
it is better
than shallow sweetness

Christmas Day

REPORT ON A BIRTH (Titus 3.4–7)

To the fidgeting infant she gave quietly
a promise into his makeshift cradle
overwhelmed with love the light which she
shed over him is still alight today
unseemingly most of the time
small like the body of a little human child
she made herself
God
could now be touched regaled and cared for
the baby grew up went his way
until the bitter end that was a beginning
for many

Boxing Day

MIRACLE AT CHRISTMAS (John 8.12)

That you are not only light
but also shadow cooling dew
in the dawn

That you are not only words
but also silence lingering distance
in a narrow glance

That you are not far away
but connected found a dwelling
in a heart pitted with scars

New Year's Eve

LONELY NEW YEAR'S EVE

Letting the old year slide away
into God's distant skies pain false hopes
missed opportunities not to be covered up
with false jolliness clattering TV laughter
simply listening into darkness time stumbling
for a moment then jumping with courage streaming on
into the new the unknown the beautiful perhaps who knows

No big deal
simply time to time

New Year's Day

SIMPLY

tired of big words
I am
looking back looking forward
resolutions to be good
simply
welcome
the new year
this quiet morning
with joy

Epiphany

TRACES OF GOD

In hands you show yourself
sometimes
baking bread
wiping away tears
meshing a net
warm like earth

In eyes you show yourself
sometimes
looking friendly
love shining through
gazing gently
into the depth

In women and men you show yourself
sometimes
dancing and laughing
hungry and cold
waiting for an answer
silently

Ash Wednesday

WASTELAND

Not
that it would be something new for me
not that this would be my first attempt
living
without cigarettes is possible
after a while
however not
to start again
is the problem
time opens up lots of time
the hands
without the lighter
the soul
wounded on my lips
and further
into the land beyond the mountains
seven weeks or longer
we'll see

Monday in Holy Week

RECIPE FOR SUCCESS (Matthew 26.36–44)

Those who are sad out of one's way
those who are dying out of one's mind
those who are afraid against the wall
save time wherever you can
look away what is it to me
money stock exchange computer the motto is
stay cool flexible
here today there tomorrow just not downwards
looking not to be committed
to anything who knows what
is the right thing to do nowadays
the deeper the sleep the better

Tuesday in Holy Week

SOMETIMES (Matthew 26.69–74)

Sometimes I do not see
your beauty
do not hear
your sound
do not feel anything
of you God

Sometimes I do not say
what I think
do not do
what I could
do not stick up
for you God

Sometimes I do not seek
your ways
do not believe in
your faithfulness
sometimes my fear is stronger
than you God

Wednesday in Holy Week

SHE HOWEVER REMAINED SILENT
(John 18.28–40; 19.1–16)

In memory of the French beguine and mystic Marguerite Porète

Open and clearly she had spoken
freely and out of her own strength talked about God
the one who is captivating both far and near as she had put it
this flowing and all penetrating love
in which she had drowned
the people listened to her wondered
and the truth of God shone around her

This came to the ears of the high priests they went to the bishop
and he went to the grand inquisitor
the woman was accused and put to trial
and interrogated about the matter
she however remained silent
as she did not want to recant did not defend herself
did not even reply to the gentlemen
she was pronounced guilty
the crowd which had been on her side yesterday
now wanted to see blood
it was all right with the king with the church anyway
the mob cajoled and laughed some cried as she was burnt on the stake
she however remained silent

Maundy Thursday

QUESTIONS OF A READING CHRISTIAN WOMAN
(Mark 14.17–26; John 13.1–15)

Who baked the bread where were
the women disciples and who set the table
at that last and first Lord's Supper
Who washed whose feet then did the men
also serve women and why and when
did they stop doing that why is a man's blood
precious that of a woman however impure what made
the Eucharist bony and shallow how can we
begin to taste God's love anew and be satisfied
through sharing?

Good Friday

WAR LAMENT

God
cries in the woman on her knees in the mud
above her only a plastic canopy
God
cries in the child there in the basement it is burning
bombs falling everywhere
God
is silent in the lies and phrases
of the eloquent language of death
God
dies

Holy Saturday

COURAGE TO DEATH (Matthew 27.61)

In silence they were sitting there and waiting
for nothing there was nothing left absolutely nothing
no explanations good perspectives or euphemisms
just a dead body nothing else
the enthusiasts turned up their sensitive noses
and turned away from the deadly truth
the smart-alecks were lost for words
when they saw him his limbs strangely twisted coagulated
blood everywhere who would not want to
run away but those two simply stayed
and of course they were women who stuck it out there
sat down in front of the grave cried they already knew that
sometimes there was nothing to be done but one had to
stay nevertheless simply stick it out together not to leave them
alone better then nothing
Where did they know that from?
Good question

Easter Vigil

OVER NIGHT

Cried the tears
said the pains
viewed the scars
the head empty and tired

now let us sleep and wait
for nothing
sometimes
only sometimes why only can
God turn over the leaf
over night

Easter Day

LITTLE EASTER

Stones
turned away from the heart
ice
thawed from the soul
hunger
turned into bread
walls broken through
into the light

Monday in Easter Week

HARD TO SAY (1 Corinthians 15.51–52)

if God can turn all pains into joy
really all of them and dry away the tears
even mine and if her power includes even death
hard to say
if mother earth will open and let the dead
go free born a second time and God will at last
become all in all and what that will mean then
hard to say

Ascension Day

WITHDRAWAL (Luke 24.50–53)

They would have liked to
keep you
secure you once and for all
measure your mystery and calculate it
multiply by three divided by seven
compress your life into the book of books
and pour your light into their picture of the world

I too would have liked God to have
found you forever
explored your depths climbed your heights
understood who you are just once
to be able to grasp you
you however hide yourself with darkness and light
behind the clouds
you catch my eye open my heart
and move on

Pentecost/Whitsun Day

PEACE HYMN (Acts 2.1–18)

O come thou peaceful Spirit
and all your strength unfold
our courage and our zest increase
as you our hopes uphold
Destroy death's bitter logic
of hatred violence war
and rouse our numbing lethargy
that life may conquer more

O come thou Spirit of the truth
enlighten this dark night
enter into hearts and mouths
the Word that clears our sight
Help us in all languages
each other's hearts to know
that we in spite of hate and fear
the way of peace may go

Tune: Ich dank Dir lieber Herre (Redeemed, restored, forgiven)

Monday after Pentecost

MIRACLE OF PENTECOST (1 Corinthians 12.4–11)

The raucous ones listen to
God in silence
The ones without a voice sing
hymns of joy
The cynics dream
visions of hope
The shy ones learn
words of courage
Women and men speak
the language of heaven

Trinity Sunday

ALL-ONE (Romans 11.36)

You the One in the waving green of the plane trees in front of my
    window
You the Not-One in the mirror of darkness emptiness in the core of
    my fear
You the Manifold-One in your sweet habitations
You breathing wide open ground openly hidden
You centre of the sun fabric of life
You source of all love
You Holy Name how precious is your trace

Harvest Festival

HARVEST FESTIVAL OF WORDS (Isaiah 58.7–12)

At the right time
you let the words grow
and thrust roots with your song
in the wasteland of silence

Sown with tears
reaped with pain
I share the fruits of my desire
break the bread of hunger
for life

My heart
expands into the wide open space
of your strength
I give room
in the darkness of my sadness
your light breaks forth

All Souls' Day

IN THE END (Psalm 90.12)

In the end
it will be very different
from what we believe
and possibly easier
than we dared hope

In the end
we will know
what really counts
and what matters
in life and death

In the end
even for me
the borders will open
and in spite of all my fear
I will jump
into the radiant You

List of Biblical References